My Friend Josh has Dyspraxia

Copyright

Title: My Friend Josh

Author: Christine Draper

Editor: Ruth-Abigail Williams

Illustrator: Antonella Cammarano

Published: achieve2day, Slough, 2017
ISBN: 978-1-909986-19-0

Dedication

This book is dedicated to my clever, creative, dyspraxic son.

This is my friend Josh. He loves to laugh and act silly, just like me! After we became good friends, I found out that he has a condition called dyspraxia. It doesn't change how much I like being his friend; it just means that some things that are simple for me, like writing with a pencil, are difficult for him. Some people with dyspraxia struggle more than others.

At first it didn't make sense to me that while Josh is better than me at maths, he was awful at colouring in – and really hated it. He also found it hard to play with lots of toys. I thought playing and colouring were much easier than maths, but Mum explained that dyspraxia affects his coordination. Coordination is the ability to make your arms, legs, and other body parts move in a controlled way. Now, I know that dyspraxia affects everyone differently and it does not mean we can't have fun, we just need to use our imaginations more.

One of the first things you might notice about Josh is that his speech isn't very clear. Josh tells me that a lot of children who have dyspraxia can talk normally like I can and it doesn't affect their speech at all. However, it definitely affected Josh's speech. When he started school no-one could understand him at all, not even his Mum! So the other children would not include him in any of their activities. It made Josh sad when the other kids made fun of him when he tried to speak.

I'm really glad Josh's speech has become much better since he started school because he makes me laugh. Even though his speech is much better, when he gets upset, it gets a bit worse again. He still has to go to speech therapy too, where someone specially trained helps Josh to talk. It makes it much easier to understand Josh now and we can make up lots of great stories. The other children in our class are much more patient too and will wait and listen when Josh puts up his hand. This makes me happy.

Josh hates sport. This is because dyspraxia really affects how well someone can move. It was really cool on Sports' Day last year. We all had to be in a race, even Josh. All the other children in his race finished in less than half the time Josh did. I started clapping and cheering him on. The rest of the school joined in, and the parents too. This really helped Josh and he was glad he kept going to the end. However, sport is definitely not his favourite subject at school.

The other subject that Josh hates because of his dyspraxia is art. His drawings look like my baby sister's. Mum says it's not fair to compare because my sister, Rosie, doesn't have dyspraxia like Josh does.

Josh has some great ideas though and he can always explain his drawings. He says that he has met someone with dyspraxia who can draw brilliantly. I didn't understand how, but he said it can affect using small muscles, like writing and drawing; or bigger muscles in the arms and legs like running and jumping or both. For Josh it's definitely both. However, he's still practicing his drawing and is even making his own comic strip!

At school, Josh uses a laptop to write. This makes a lot of our class jealous, including me. The teachers say his work is much better when he uses a laptop. He writes the most amazing stories, as he has a great imagination. No-one would be able to read them if he wrote them by hand. Josh says that his Mum made him practice his handwriting every night for years and he hated it. I think using a laptop is much better. Josh agrees.

I remember when we were little, lunch time used to be a problem too. Josh couldn't eat properly with a knife and fork and would always get food all over himself. Sometimes, I used to try to clean him up, but other times he would run off when other kids would call him names. He still brings in a packed lunch to school.

When Josh was little his Dad would get annoyed with him. Then his Dad saw him with his occupational therapist, which is someone who helps him to move better. He could see that Josh was trying really hard but just couldn't do it. He has improved but whenever I have Josh over, we always have pizza because it's easy for Josh to eat. I don't mind because I love pizza.

Another problem with meals and in class at school is that Josh is always fidgeting with something. He finds it hard to stay seated and is always fiddling with his clothing, a pen, headphones, the fabric on the chair, all sorts of strange things. He even destroyed his sister's piano stool by picking at it. His sister, Verity, was not happy.

I really like helping Josh. A lot of people think that dyspraxia is only about how well people move, but it can really affect Josh's ability to organise himself too. I help him pack up his books after class, arrange his P.E. kit and remind him about things he has forgotten. His class teacher also helps a lot. She has learned to be patient with him in class and never yells at him. This has helped Josh to improve. Helping Josh makes me think of helping take care of my sister, Rosie, at home. I love that too.

Josh's Mum and Dad say that he is better at looking after himself at home too. Though his Dad does find his short term memory really frustrating. It's just part of dyspraxia for many people though. And his mum is still always telling him to put his tops on the right way round. "Look here's the label - that should go at the back," she says. Now he sometimes even gets his own cereal in the morning ... and without most of it ending on the floor.

Josh does not like getting his hair cut! This is because he has sensory processing disorder or SPD for short. To Josh, this makes getting his haircut feel really horrible. Sometimes his hair gets super long and bushy. Then the school gets upset and his parents make him go to the barber. I don't mind his hair long, he looks like a rock star in a band! The SPD also makes Josh sensitive to some materials. Josh never wears jeans because they feel uncomfortable on his skin. Josh says that a lot of people have SPD as a part of their dyspraxia.

I have lots of fun making up stories with Josh. He is good at English and loves reading. Many children with dyspraxia also have dyslexia. Dyslexia is a condition that can cause problems with reading, writing and spelling. People with dyslexia commonly confuse the order of letters in words, mix up words that sound the same but are spelled differently and write letters the wrong way around. I'm glad Josh doesn't because he wants to be an author when he grows up. It's good that he likes writing stories because some of the things I like doing with my other friends, like riding our bikes, Josh can't do.

I like being Josh's friend but Josh doesn't have many friends. This is because while Josh is not autistic he does have autistic tendencies. Autistic tendencies just means that he's not very good at being friends with other children. The school used to try and get him to participate in different group activities, but Josh is really happy being on his own. His mum says that it's just part of his dyspraxia. Some children with dyspraxia do have autism too, though many do not. While it is common to have both autism and dyspraxia, they are different conditions. I would like to find out more about autism sometime, wouldn't you?

When he was little, Josh used to be really jealous of his big sister, Verity. Verity used to get lots of party invites and play dates and he had none. Now he doesn't want any because he really doesn't like parties. He did come to my last party but after half an hour he was pulling on his Mum's sleeve asking if they could go home yet. I think it's odd not to like parties, don't you?

Josh has had lots of therapy. He has had years of occupational therapy, OT for short, and lots of speech therapy too. This means that while Josh still has difficulty with many things, he is much better than he used to be. He has also learned how to manage too. For example, he always wears shoes with Velcro fastenings, as he cannot tie his shoelaces.

I'm glad I have Josh as a friend as it has taught me about dyspraxia and that it is worthwhile to make friends with people that are a little bit different. So I decided to look up dyspraxia on the computer. I had to ask Mum how to spell it! I found out that about one in 30 children have some form of dyspraxia, though only a few have it as severe as Josh. It is much more common in boys than girls, though girls can have it too. I learned that you cannot grow out of dyspraxia, so Josh will have it for life. I also found out that there is no known cause. Maybe I will be able to find out the cause when I am older.

CPSIA information can be obtained
at www.ICGtesting.com
Printed in the USA
LVHW07s1838280318
571476LV00020B/266/P